GIANTS WILL FALL

DUTCH SHEETS

Become A History Maker And Take Out The Goliaths

GIANTS WILL FALL

DUTCH SHEETS

Published by Dutch Sheets Ministries
P.O. Box 63359
Colorado Springs, CO 80962
www.DutchSheets.org

Printed in the United States of America

ISBN 978-0-692-05863-3

Cover design by Breanna Renteria

TABLE OF CONTENTS

Introduction 7

PART 1
The Mission

Chapter 1 11
Pioneering Hebron

Chapter 2 17
America's Downward Spiral

Chapter 3 25
Making History

Chapter 4 33
The Cause

PART 2
The Weapons

Chapter 5 43
The Gloves

Chapter 6 51
Using History As Our Weapon

Chapter 7 57
David's History

Chapter 8 65
America's History

Chapter 9 71
Kingly Intercession

Endnotes 79

INTRODUCTION

I have become convinced that the earth is about to experience the greatest revival in history. I actually believe we may see more people won to Christ in the next 20 years than we have in the previous 2000.

America will be used greatly in this harvest. We continue to play a significant role in the world, both naturally and spiritually. Satan has tried desperately to hinder America's destiny by producing compromise, a departure from our Christian roots, and grievous sins resulting in defilement and devastating curses.

God, however, keeps covenant and mercy to a thousand generations (see Deuteronomy 7:9) and the purpose for which he raised up America—the preaching of the gospel to every nation—is still intact. Holy Spirit is going to resurrect this calling by sending another Great Awakening and by enabling us to overthrow the spiritual strongholds now ruling America.

In 2007, a young man with whom I am acquainted was given an interesting dream involving the pulling down of spiritual strongholds in America. In the dream, I was a boxer, knocking out giants. I represented the prayer movement in America; the giants, of course, represented *spiritual* giants. I believe we are living in the season of the dream's fulfillment! Just as David defeated Goliath, the praying church is about to take out the "giants" now ruling America, restoring our nation to its God-given purpose and destiny.

In 2015 I wrote the book *An Appeal to Heaven* which makes the case that God is not finished with America, and that the same spiritual activity He used to birth this great nation will be employed to restore it: prayer. *Giants Will Fall* is a sequel, of sorts, focusing on the new phase of this prayer movement.

The worldwide prayer movement will go to new levels in 2018. Just as the glory in the church is increasing, so, too, is our ability to express the fullness of Christ on earth. Jesus has promised to build a glorious church (Ephesians 5:27), one the very gates of hell won't overcome (Matthew 16:18). A new expression of this maturing Church will now begin to manifest. As it does, giants will fall…the church will arise…and the power of the gospel will be seen in all its splendor.

Be encouraged.

PART I

THE MISSION

CHAPTER 1

PIONEERING HEBRON

"I've heard a word from God," Chuck Pierce told me. I was excited. Chuck is a prophet, after all. What pearl of wisdom was he about to share with me? Directions for my future? A profound nugget of revelation? If nothing truly spiritual, perhaps at least something exciting, like who would win the Super Bowl.

Don't laugh—he's done that before.

I was expectant. We were in Israel, the place where Jesus had lived and ministered. Chuck probably tapped into the timing of Christ's return to earth, or maybe who the anti-Christ is. Who knows what he had picked up from the revelation-filled airwaves of Jerusalem!

"I heard Holy Spirit say, 'I'm going to pioneer Hebron again,'" he stated with a great deal of confidence.

I, in return, gave him a mix of "deer in headlights" and "you've got to be kidding" looks. "What does that mean?" I asked the prophet.

"I don't know."

"What do you mean you don't know? You're a prophet, for crying out loud," I reminded him.

"Well, I heard Holy Spirit say it, but I don't know what it means," he stated. "I think it's for you. He'll tell you what it means."

Prophets can be annoying.

I wasn't completely surprised. Chuck has done this to me before. God will sometimes give him a word or phrase—just enough to entice me. I, then, have to discern for myself what it means. It must be a game God and prophets sometimes play with us normal folks.

So I locked in on Hebron.

The names of people and places in Old Testament times were important, their meanings often holding prophetic significance. Bethel, for example, where Jacob had a profound encounter with God, means "the house of God." Jerusalem means "the city of peace or wholeness." Hebron—the place Holy Spirit said He would pioneer again—means "friendship." It also means "league, confederacy, or federation." Though the word itself doesn't refer to a covenant, the concept is certainly there. "Hebron" is a strong alliance born out of a close relationship. Because of this meaning, God made it the final resting place of Abraham, the covenantal friend of God. With this meaning in mind, Hebron became symbolic of several things:

- It is the highest city in Israel; therefore, covenantal friendship with God is the "highest" or most lofty privilege we are afforded. It is also the thing satan most wants to steal.
- Hebron was the city where King David first set up his throne. Authority is released as we walk in intimacy and covenantal friendship with God.
- Later in Israel's development, Hebron became one of its "Cities of Refuge." These were cities structured and managed to protect individuals who had accidentally taken a person's life. The individuals fled to a city of refuge in order to prevent a family member of the slain person from

enacting revenge. It was inconvenient, but better than vengeance killings. Later, the New Testament tells us these cities of refuge became types or pictures of Christ, to whom we "have fled for refuge" (Hebrews 6:18, KJV). Hebron, then, pictures the safety and refuge we find in Christ.

Satan hates geographical locations that have become meaningful to God and His people. When possible, he seeks to defile them, using perversions, violence, covenant breaking, idolatry, and the shedding of innocent blood. Hebron, as a type of Christ and a picture of covenantal friendship with God, became a prime target, and in the four centuries between Abraham and Joshua, evil giants had overtaken the city. In fact, the greatest of all the Anakim (giants), Arba, made it his stronghold, and renamed Hebron after himself: Kiriath-arba, meaning "the city of Arba" (see Joshua 14:15).

By the time the 12 spies of Israel were sent by Moses to check out the Promised Land, three more giants, direct descendants of Anak from whom the giants were spawned, had inherited Hebron (see Numbers 13:22, 28, 33). This holy place, representing friendship and covenant with God, was now ruled by giants and was a place of terror. It so terrified ten of the twelve spies, in fact, that they brought back an evil report of fear and unbelief to the rest of the nation. "There is no way we can take our promised land," they stated. "The giants are simply too big and powerful."

Caleb, one of the 12 spies, was indignant. Seeing that Arba and the other giants had defiled this holy city and desecrated the final resting place of the patriarch Abraham, he was angry. His response was to ask Moses for this very mountain top city as his inheritance. "We can conquer these giants and their fortified cities, guys," Caleb told the fearful Israelites, "and I'll take the biggest." Because of the Israelites' fear and unbelief, however, Caleb had to wait for this opportunity. Forty-five years later, after 40 years of wilderness wandering by the unbelieving generation and another 5 years of war, it was time. Caleb, now 85 years old, said, "Give me my mountain!" (Joshua 14:12). In asking for this piece of land, this warrior was asking for more than a city; he was requesting the assignment of conquering the greatest stronghold of the giants.

Caleb was BAD.

The great warrior did, indeed, conquer Kiriath-arba and its giants, then renamed it Hebron. In the words of my prophetic friend, *he pioneered Hebron again.* In that special place, Caleb enjoyed covenantal friendship with God. He also paved the way for it to become David's first capital and a picture of Christ, our Savior and our Refuge.

When Holy Spirit declared through Chuck that He was going to "pioneer Hebron again," He was making an encouraging and wonderful announcement: "I am going to empower you to confront and take out spiritual giants ruling regions of the earth, transforming these regions into strongholds of life. You are going to transform spiritually dark cities and nations into places where covenantal friendship with God can be experienced, and from which the rule and authority of Christ—He who sits on the throne of David—can be seen again.

I did my happy dance!

A New Era

This book is about knocking out giants, taking them down once and for all. The church is moving into a new era. We will soon experience our finest and most productive season of harvesting souls. I believe we, the body of Christ, will see at least a *billion* souls saved in the next 10-20 years, perhaps more than have been saved in the previous 2000! Portions of the earth that have been ruled by evil, spiritual giants will be liberated. Evil forces have ruled some regions since Adam's fall. But there is a holy invasion about to occur, a release of Caleb-hearted, fearless warriors who will thrill at the thought of conquering cities for Christ.

Enlist!

Ask for your mountain!

In the prayer movement, we have a distinct role to play in birthing this new era. *All that God does on Earth is birthed through His intercessors.* The goal of this book is to bring understanding of your weapons, to strengthen your faith regarding knocking out spiritual giants, and to give instruction on how to do this. The praying Church is about to step into its highest authority, and its greatest history-writing role.

CHAPTER 2

AMERICA'S DOWNWARD SPIRAL

In the 1970's, Don McLean wrote a song about America and it was one of the most popular songs of his day. American Pie was listed by the Recording Industry Association of America as the number 5 song of the 20th century.[1] A notable and favorite line of this oldie is "the day the music died."[2] McLean was more prophetic than he knew. "The land of the free" has become the land of the bound. *America the Beautiful* still describes us on the outside. Internally, however, we are ugly, ravaged by societal disease and moral decay. *Like Hebron, we have become a stronghold of giants.*

In their desire to be encouragers, many religious leaders refuse to point out the true condition of America. I get it. No one wants to bring discouragement and, to be sure, a critical spirit and defeatist attitude must be guarded against. But no serious doctor would begin treating a patient without first diagnosing the problem. To blindly declare that everything will be okay, simply because God is good and gracious, is beyond naive; it is untrue. An accurate diagnosis is not only sound wisdom, it is compassion.

While not blind to America's condition, I am not discouraged. In pointing out America's desperate need, I do not want to discourage you; I want to awaken and motivate you. Like Caleb, I am indignant and ready to take out some giants. America is in trouble and very sick, but NOT terminal. Let's take an honest look at our true condition.

America's Condition

God, who was pushed from our hearts by the giants of pride, materialism, humanism and pleasure, was inevitably also expelled from our schools, government, and the core of American life. The results have been shocking. To date, we have murdered almost 60 million babies in what should be their safe haven of nourishment and development.[3] We harvest their organs and sell their body parts.[4] *This is celebrated!* Protecting animals and trees is considered noble and praiseworthy; fighting for the unborn is deemed a sign of intolerance and bigotry.

Unimaginable.

Isaiah prophesied this lunacy: "The people will be oppressed, every one by another and every one by his neighbor; the child will be insolent towards the elder, and *the base toward the honorable*" (Isaiah 3:5, NKJV, emphasis added). In our baseness, we now actually crush the skull of a half-born baby, and then finish the birth process of the now murdered corpse.[5] Let that sink in. Sadly, it is today's America. This brutal procedure, called partial-birth abortion, is "justified" because the feet aren't yet out of the womb. Utter madness. The history we are writing is heartbreaking.

Mothers, fathers, national leaders, and even some in the church fight for this "right" and consider it noble freedom-fighting. The winner-take-all lust of today's giants is insatiably feeding on our offspring, our very flesh and blood. For these babies, the music most certainly died, but their blood still cries out from our land. Few are listening. After 45 years, America's shameful and heinous holocaust continues. *God, forgive us.*

Where did we go wrong? How did the love of life die and give way to such insanity? How can we kill the child we once would have died for? May God have mercy on our depraved society.

The Youth of America

Our children now follow our disregard for life, killing one another and themselves. Consider these alarming statistics in America:

- Suicide is now the second leading cause of death in young people. Over 5,000 commit suicide every year—more than 13 each day.[6]
- Child protective services is able to substantiate the claim of a sexual assault on a teenager every 8 minutes. That is 180 confirmed assaults *every day*. And conservative estimates say 2 out of 3 assaults are never reported.[7]
- 719 teenage girls undergo abortions every day – roughly 262,500 each year.[8]
- Roughly 10 million new sexually transmitted diseases and infections occur in teens every year in this country. These diseases, many of them causing sterility and some even death, have become another ploy of satan to wipe out a generation.[9]

Life has been cheapened. Greed and selfishness rule; sacrifice is out. Authority is mocked while rebellion and violence are extolled by our so-called role models and heroes. "If it feels good, do it" is now more than an overused cliché—it is a terrifying reality. When suggested that allowing God back into our schools might help, smugness and defiant arrogance are often the responses of those who so desperately want Him banned.

Satan's insidious attack on the home has borne fruit. During the twentieth century, the divorce rate rose 700 percent in America. Thirteen million children under the age of 18 are growing up with one or both parents away from home. Seventy percent of all juveniles in state reform institutions come from fatherless homes.[10] We wonder why young people grow disillusioned and dysfunctional. They're the product of our rebellion. They are simply reaping what we have shamefully sown.

Other signs point to our true condition. We are a nation of addicts and lawless rebels. The United States is the single largest market on the earth for illegal drugs, and leads the world in the export of pornography.[11] We cannot build prisons fast enough to hold our criminals. We're rich in goods and poor in character—powerful without, weak and self-destructive within. America's music has become horribly discordant, yet we're so tone deaf we don't notice. Our wealth and power have anesthetized us to our true condition; we're bleeding to death internally, while continuing to party on.

The Struggling Church

What about the Church in America, God's intended salt and light for this mess? Many Christian leaders think we're doing a pretty good job of reaching our nation—probably due to the relatively new phenomenon of mega churches—but do the facts support this? Consider the following:

- Since 2007, Christianity in the United States has decreased by about 8%.[12]
- Church attendance and Bible reading are at decreased levels of involvement. (My note: This means we have actually lost ground.)[13]
- Six out of 10 Americans believe "the Holy Spirit is a symbol of God's power or presence but is not a living entity."[14]

- One out of every five professing to be born-again Christians believes the Bible contains errors.[15]
- Rather than following Jesus' exhortation to be "in the world but not of it," today's Christians seem to thirst for the opposite reality—to be inseparable from the world, while somehow retaining the aura of devout followers of Christ.
- Only 44 percent of born-again Christians are certain of the absoluteness of moral truth.[16]

Our Denial Must End

Things are shockingly out of control, and like Arba, Hebron's demonic conqueror, the giants in our land are mocking us in the name of their gods. Every part of American society is screaming for cause-minded, impassioned followers of Christ to arise and help resurrect our song. As Nehemiah observed about his nation, our walls are down and our gates burned (see Nehemiah 1:3). Hosea's description of ancient Israel is also appropriate—we have sown the wind and are reaping the whirlwind (see Hosea 8:7).

It is past time to abandon our denial. Many Americans are like the optimist Mark Twain wrote of. Describing a fight he was obviously losing, this denial expert bragged, "Thrusting my nose firmly between his teeth, I threw him heavily to the ground on top of me."[17]

Good ol' American optimism.

We, in America, especially the body of Christ, must wake up to our true condition. We have become the proverbial frog in the kettle—we're dying and don't know it. Like the band on the *RMS Titanic*, we continue playing while the ship is sinking. Our propensity for only treating the symptoms is foolish and futile. We cannot bail the water fast enough.

You will clearly see as you read this book, that I still have great hope for America. Our song CAN be resurrected. For hope and optimism to be legitimate, however, they must exist in the light of reality. Otherwise, they are nothing more than denial-driven complacency. In our misguided optimism, we have, like the causeless army of Israel when facing Goliath, convinced ourselves that if we wait long enough, the shocking giants of the land will go away and leave us alone.

This will never happen!

We Have Promises to Claim

Satan has no intention of letting up in his relentless assault on America. Positive change will only come when a people of passion, like Caleb, rise to the challenge and meet the enemy in battle. If we do, we can turn the tide. Though our condition is critical, consider these comforting promises:

> "Yet even now," declares the LORD, "return to Me with all your heart and with fasting, weeping, and mourning; and rend your heart and not your garments. Now return to the LORD your God, for He is gracious and compassionate, slow to anger, abounding in loving-kindness, and relenting of evil. Who knows whether He will not turn and relent, and leave a blessing behind Him (Joel 2:12-14)?

> Come let us return to the LORD. For He has torn us, but He will heal us: He has wounded us, but He will bandage us. He will revive us after two days; He will raise us up on the third day that we may live before Him. So let us know, let us press on to know the LORD. His going forth is as certain as the dawn; and He will come to us as the rain, like the spring rain watering the earth (Hosea 6:1-3).

> Fear not, for you will not be put to shame, neither feel humiliated, for you will not be disgraced; but you will

forget the shame of your youth, and the reproach of your widowhood you will remember no more (Isaiah 54:4).

Instead of your shame you will have a double portion, and instead of humiliation they will shout for joy over their portion. Therefore they will possess a double portion in their land (Isaiah 61:7).

Repentance of sin, turning back to God, and a Third Great Awakening are America's only hope. Will this occur? Will we see the fulfillment of these and other hope-filled promises? YES! Modern day Caleb's—bold, cause-minded spiritual warriors—are arising.

In their book *Is It Real When It Doesn't Work?* Doug Murren and Bard Shurin recount:

Toward the end of the nineteenth century, Swedish chemist Alfred Nobel awoke one morning to read his own obituary in the local newspaper: "Alfred Nobel, the inventor of dynamite, who died yesterday, devised a way for more people to be killed in a war than ever before, and he died a rich man."

Actually, it was Alfred's older brother who had died; a newspaper reporter had bungled the epitaph. But the account had a profound effect on Nobel. He decided he wanted to be known for something other than developing the means to kill people efficiently and for amassing a fortune in the process. So he initiated the Nobel Prize, the award for scientists and writers who foster peace.

Nobel said, "Every man ought to have the chance to correct his epitaph in midstream and write a new one."[18]

Profound. And worth emulating.

God is giving America a chance to re-write her epitaph. If written today, it would read, "Weighed in the Balances and Found Wanting," or perhaps, "The Giants Won." But our gracious and merciful God, slow to anger and abounding in loving-kindness, forgives sinners and heals nations.

And to cause-minded Caleb's…He gives anointings to slay giants.

You, my friend, are a giant slayer.

CHAPTER 3

MAKING HISTORY

Several years ago I was gripped by a thought Holy Spirit dropped into my heart: *You can either watch history being made or you can make it.* He wasn't referring to becoming famous, of course, but to shaping history. I decided to become one of the history *makers*, not just a watcher.

During World War II, England needed to increase its production of coal. Winston Churchill called together labor leaders to enlist their support. At the end of his presentation he asked them to picture in their minds a parade, which he knew would be held in Piccadilly Circus after the war. First, he said, would come the sailors who had kept the vital sea-lanes open. Then would come the soldiers who had come home from Dunkirk and then gone on to defeat Rommel in Africa. Then would come the pilots who had driven the Luftwaffe from the sky.

Last of all, he said, would come a long line of sweat-stained, soot-streaked men in miner's caps. Someone would cry from the crowd, "And where were you during the critical days of our struggle?"

And from ten thousand throats would come the answer, "We were deep in the earth with our faces to the coal."[1]

We can't all be famous, but our involvement matters, and is crucial!

I love the song *History Maker*, written by another British man named Martin Smith, the former lead singer for the U.K. Christian band, Delirious. The lyrics speak of the power of prayer, of cloudless skies breaking forth with rain, of miraculous healings, and broken-hearted people becoming history makers. If you've never heard it, Google it. I think you'll like it.

A few years back, knowing my love for the song and my desire to truly make a difference in America, a friend gave me a nice pen inscribed with "History Maker." When all is said and done, will I actually be one? We'll know in 20 or 30 years. If not, I can assure you it will not be from lack of effort.

Actually, in another sense (and this may surprise you) the question isn't really whether or not I, or anyone else, will be a history maker; we're all participating in the history-making process. The real questions—which we are all answering with our lives—are: 1) *what* history are we writing? And 2) will we write it *intentionally* or by default? We all shape history, one way or another.

Facing the Giant

When David was about to face the giant, Goliath, his older brother was mocking him regarding what seemed like such a preposterous idea. David's response was the poignant question,

"Is there not a cause?" (1 Samuel 17:29). Would it come as a surprise if I told you the word "cause" also means "history?"[2] David was also very possibly asking his brother and fellow Israelites the question "Is there not a history?" He could have been thinking of past history, which we will discuss later, but it is entirely possible David was thinking of the future—a history to write. *"Come on guys,"* David may have been imploring, *"history will record what we do here today. Will we go down in history as giant-killers or cowards? Will we fight for God and country or will we flee? Don't allow this giant to define us; let faith in God define us!"*

Interestingly, Goliath's name actually comes from a root word meaning "to expose or reveal."[3] How appropriate. Giants of adversity will most assuredly reveal our nature. Are we a David? A Caleb? Or, like Israel's soldiers who fled from Goliath, are we cowards? David refused to be defined by cowardice. He chose, rather, to be defined by a cause.

The choices we must make to write a godly history are not always easy. Complacency often seems to be the easiest route, but it can also be the most destructive. As the following example illustrates, the path of least resistance can sometimes be fatal.

> For years, the opening of "The Wide World of Sports" television program illustrated "the agony of defeat" with a painful ending to an attempted ski jump. The skier appeared in good form as he headed down the jump, but then, for no apparent reason, tumbled head over heels off the side of the jump, bouncing off the supporting structure in the process.
>
> What viewers didn't know was that he *chose* to fall rather than finish the jump. Why? As he explained later, the jump surface had become too fast. Midway down the ramp, he realized if he completed the jump he

would land on the level ground beyond the safe, sloped landing area, which could have been fatal.

As it was, the skier suffered no more than a headache from the tumble.[4]

At this time in our history, America must leave the seemingly safe ski slope. I believe that is what the 2016 presidential elections were about. We were racing to our destruction and the course correction was radical, but necessary. The alternative was to have become permanently enslaved to the giants of our day.

America's Destiny

God not only desires to save us politically, however; He also wants to fully restore America's spiritual purpose and destiny. Our purpose as a nation is to partner with Christ, just as Israel did, becoming a light to the nations. Our divine calling is to spread the gospel of Jesus Christ from these shores to the ends of the earth. And it is to be an example of what Jehovah will do for a nation "whose God is the Lord" (Psalms 33:12).

With America's deterioration of the past 40-50 years, this calling has been in jeopardy. Rather than exporting the gospel, we are now the leading exporter of pornography, as well as other forms of depravity through film and music.[5] America is literally trafficking in filth! Portions of the shocking history we are writing today will one day shame us.

We experiment on aborted babies and sell their body parts without shame, referring to them as "fetal tissue."[6] Transferring babies from the womb to the organ bank or dumpster is now a deplorably shocking part of American history. The madness must stop! We're writing a nauseating history, one over which our children and grandchildren will weep. But as the following example shows us, the dirge can become a song of victory.

The name Norma McCorvey probably doesn't mean anything to you. But the pseudonym Norma McCorvey used in the landmark Supreme Court case in which she was the plaintiff you will probably recognize. She was Jane Roe, of *Roe versus Wade*, and the infamous decision in 1973 that legalized abortion on demand.

According to Kathleen Donnelly, in 1969 Norma McCorvey was working as a barker for a traveling carnival when she discovered she was pregnant. She asked a doctor to give her an abortion and was surprised to find it was against the law. She sought help elsewhere and was recruited as the plaintiff in Roe versus Wade by two attorneys seeking to overturn the law against abortion. Ironically, because the case took four years to be finally decided, McCorvey never was able to abort the child and instead gave her baby up for adoption.

She remained anonymous for a decade or so, and then Norma McCorvey went public. Donnelly writes:

Shaking, sick to her stomach and fortified by vodka and Valium—she told a Dallas television reporter she was Jane Roe of Roe v. Wade….next, she admitted she had lied about that pregnancy in the hope it would help her get an abortion: it was a casual affair that made her pregnant, not rape as she told her Roe lawyers. And, little by little, through occasional interviews, sporadic speaking engagements and a 1989 television movie, she revealed that before she gave birth to the Roe baby and gave her to adoptive parents, she had given birth to two other children….Slowly, she began speaking of her long-term lesbian relationship….[Her memoir I am Roe] leaves little out: not her childhood of petty crime and reform school, or the affairs with lovers of both sexes, or the long nights spent drinking in Dallas dives, or the days of low-level drug-dealing that preceded Roe.

According to writer Jeff Hooten in Citizen, McCorvey soon went to work answering phones for a Dallas abortion clinic. Next door to the clinic the pro-life group Operation Rescue leased an office. After a time, Norma began to have a change of heart. One day she began referring callers to Operation Rescue. Hooten writes:

Her turning point came when a 7-year-old girl named Emily—the daughter of an Operation Rescue volunteer who greeted McCorvey each day with a hug—invited McCorvey to church. On July 22, 1995, McCorvey attended a Saturday night church service in Dallas. "Norma just kept praying, 'I want to undo all the evil I've done in this world,'" said Ronda Mackey, Emily's mother. "She was crying, and you knew it was so sincere."

In August of 1995 she announced she had become a Christian and was baptized in a swimming pool in front of ABC "World News Tonight" television cameras. For a short time she said she still supported abortions in the first trimester, but before long that conviction fell by the wayside. Says McCorvey, "I still feel very badly. I guess I always will...but I know I've been forgiven."[7]

Norma, whom satan used to help write one of the ugliest chapters in American history, was rescued and is now in heaven. America, too, will recover from this insidious evil and write a new song, a song not about death and holocaust, but about the beauty of life.

Christ Wants to Restore America

Jesus said to Jerusalem, "You did not recognize the time of your visitation" (Luke 19:44). Unfortunately, the word "visitation" does not clearly communicate what Christ had offered them. He was not simply referencing a "visit." The Greek word is *episcope*, from which we get the words "bishop," "overseer," and "superintendent." Jesus was actually saying to Jerusalem, "I came to cover you, to be your Shepherd and Protector. I wanted to take you as a mother hen would her chicks and hide you under My wings, covering and protecting you. But you did not recognize this" (see Luke 13:34).

We in America are currently receiving the same offer Christ initially made to Jerusalem. God is giving us an opportunity to return to Him and the promise of His loving care. His desire is to demonstrate that righteousness—not money, power, or pleasure—exalts a nation (see Proverbs 14:34). Jesus is knocking at America's door, asking *will you receive Me back into this nation as your Shepherd and Bishop, allowing Me to cover, protect and lead you? Will you once more become a nation under God?*

Ultimately, it will be the Church that answers those questions. "If my people," has always been the deciding factor regarding whether or not a nation is healed and blessed (see 2 Chronicles 7:14). We, the Church, must refuse to surrender this nation to humanists, atheists, liberal politicians, and individuals who want the influence of God and the Bible removed from America. Though much ground has been lost to these ungodly forces, it is not too late. All the earth belongs to God (see Psalms 24:1), and we must appeal to Him for change. Of course, we must always walk in tolerance and love. But loving people doesn't equate to giving them everything they want, nor should tolerance be confused with abdication.

Just as David did, we the Church can write a righteous history. The giants of sin and godlessness in our nation can absolutely be conquered and the hearts of people can most certainly be won. Though the taunting giants may mock us in the name of their gods, just as Goliath did Israel's army, we can daily and fervently decree biblical promises such as, "Where sin abounded, grace did much more abound" (Romans 5:20, KJV). And the great promise of 2 Chronicles 7:14 is still true today, "If my people, who are called by my name, shall humble themselves, and pray, and seek my face, and turn from their wicked ways; then will I hear from heaven, and will forgive their sin, and I will heal their land." I believe this with all my heart, and live for this hope.

We in America are not at the mercy of spiritual giants. Though the past several years have been devastating, we can write a new and glorious chapter for our nation. Let's do it! Let's humble ourselves, call upon God, and go on the offense through prayer. If we do so, confessing the sins of America and appealing to God for mercy, He will answer our prayers and pour out His Spirit on this land once again.

The giants wrote America's last chapter; let us—the praying Church—write the next one.

CHAPTER 4

THE CAUSE

He stood as a titan on the battlefield, his intimidating presence mortifying the ranks of the armies of Israel. According to one translation of scripture, Goliath was "the shock trooper."[1] This giant would have made the average NBA player look like a preschooler. Standing "six cubits and a span" (1 Samuel 17:4), somewhere near 9½ feet tall, Goliath must have appeared surreal to the Israelites. "Shocking" was no doubt an appropriate term to describe him. Twice each day—80 times in all—this gargantuan Philistine stood before them and cursed the God of Israel, causing the Israelite soldiers to cower in fear at his terrifying challenge, "Send out a man to fight me" (see 1 Samuel 17:8-10).

To David, the young shepherd-boy, however, the fact that no one had accepted Goliath's challenge was even more shocking than the giant's menacing size. After all, greater things were at stake than just this one battle. The Philistines, Israel's archenemies, were determined to conquer the people of God and eradicate them from the land. David knew that Goliath's challenge was winner-take-all!

David saw beyond Goliath's size and daunting intimidation. He knew something greater was at stake. Perhaps this is what young David was implying with the question—"Is there not a cause?"—when he announced he was going to face this giant (1 Samuel 17:29, KJV). What a probing question.

David's question implied: *There are some things more important than our individual lives. Our decision shouldn't be made based on how terrifying, imposing or indestructible this giant seems; there is a cause far bigger and far more important than the potential cost of facing this menacing giant.*

What was this "cause" David spoke of?

- The well-being of Israel's wives and children hung in the balance
- Homes and possessions were on the line
- The blood that had been shed by others to purchase their freedom was about to be trampled underfoot
- Israel's freedom was at stake
- The very purposes of God through His covenant with Abraham were in jeopardy!

The Cause of Christ

Don't read that last statement too quickly—it is loaded with significance. Goliath's challenge was about so much more than simply one nation fighting another; it concerned more than just a squabble over a few square miles of dirt. The freedoms and destiny of one nation, although very significant, cannot compare to the greater cause hidden in this drama. The very purposes of God on the earth were at stake!

God's covenant with Abraham had been initiated in order to establish a Messianic lineage, an entry point for He Himself to enter earth's fallen race and redeem the world. And this divine cause was in jeopardy. No wonder satan was fighting Israel so fervently through this demonized giant—eternity for billions of people was at stake; companionship for Father God and a Bride for His Son were on the line; the integrity and vindication of Jehovah, who promised to redeem fallen humanity, were at risk; and the recompense due satan, the destroyer, also hung in the balance.

Indeed, there was a cause!

Was David aware of all this? Perhaps not, but he certainly realized this was about more than simply the well being of Israel. God, the text tells us, was being "taunted." Goliath "cursed David *by his gods*" (1 Samuel 17: 43, 45), revealing the deeper and more subtle plot unfolding on this ancient battlefield. It was a battle between the Kingdom of God and the kingdom of satan.

Thinking of this greater cause, David, lover of God, responded with this goal in fighting the giant: "that all the earth may know there is a God in Israel, and that all this assembly may know that the LORD does not deliver by sword or by spear; for the battle is the LORD's and He will give you into our hands" (1 Samuel 17:46-47). Clearly, David understood that a cause greater than the survival of his nation was at stake...a noteworthy cause worth fighting and, if necessary, dying for.

And fight David did, killing the shock trooper and removing his head! History was made; the cause was saved and Israel's destiny protected. Such is the role of destiny-driven, cause-minded people: preserving causes and writing history.

America's destiny, like Israel of old, is being challenged. Spiritual giants are trying to abort our destiny, and in doing so, frustrate the plans of God around the world. But God is calling cause-minded warriors who perceive the situation in America clearly enough—and believe in the cause passionately enough—to become history-making, destiny-preserving giant-killers. I hope you're one of them.

America's Former Giant Killers

America, like Israel of old, has had giant-killing heroes in its past. Fighting for righteous causes and shaping history is in our DNA. I was recently inspired afresh as I re-read *The Light and the Glory*, the masterful work by Peter Marshall and David Manuel which plainly outlines God's plan and destiny for America. The book also clearly reveals the allegiance and dependence our Founding Fathers had toward God. They were God honoring, God fearing and, as the following quote illustrates, warriors at heart.

> As the Revolutionary War was about to begin, Captain John Parker called out to the seventy-odd Minutemen hastily forming a line on the Lexington green. "Stand your ground! Don't fire unless fired upon. But if they want to have a war, let it begin here![2]

Inspiring, indeed.

Unlike Parker's day, however, today's war for America has already begun and the opening volley has already been fired. Though our battle is certainly of a different nature, "we wrestle not against flesh and blood" (Ephesians 6:12, KJV), it is no less real and will be no less intense. And most certainly, as was the case in America's revolution and in Israel's battle with Goliath, the destiny of our nation and the purposes of God on earth are at stake. The looming question is: *are there enough spiritual American heroes today with the necessary commitment and passion to save our destiny?* We will soon know, for today's Goliaths have made their stand and issued their challenge. An incredible chapter of America's history is about to be written.

One of our national forefathers, Patrick Henry, in a well-known and passionate plea to his fellow Americans to fight for the cause of freedom, declared, "I know not what course others may take; but as for me, give me liberty or give me death."[3]

Sounds like David. Or Caleb.

Patrick Henry and our nation's other early warriors considered natural freedom a cause worth fighting and dying for. America's battle today involves *spiritual* freedom and the destinies of billions of souls around the world—is that not also a cause worth fighting, even dying for?

I recently read Tom Brokaw's book *The Greatest Generation*, which chronicles the enormous struggle and price paid by the World War II generation of Americans. Their selfless heroism and tenacious determination to defeat the demonized, Nazi giants of their day and preserve the cause of freedom on earth was incredibly moving. Approximately 292,000 Americans were killed in battle and 1.7 million wounded in that war.[4]

Calling For Today's Giant Killers

Just as those allied heroes, we today are facing a D-Day of our own. In this war, the *eternal* destinies of souls are at stake. Is there another great generation of *spiritual* soldiers who will storm our "Normandy"—the gates of hell—and lay it all on the line for a righteous freedom cause? Is not our *eternal* cause just as noble as was theirs?

Just as it was in David's day, God's reputation is certainly part of our cause. Is He not taunted daily in our land and cursed in the name of false gods? Are not His words and laws mocked? In the past, America, more than any other nation, has been known as an example of what it means to be a Christian nation. Our sin, however, now mocks and reproaches Him, while presenting a false picture of what a nation "under God" should look like. Our motto, "In God We Trust," is currently no more than a faith-filled statement of hope, clung to by a remnant determined to make it a national reality once again. For those who know and love Him, this should be one of our motivating causes.

Am I being overly dramatic in making such shocking comparisons and assertions? *Come on, Sheets,* I can almost hear some thinking. *Is America's destiny really at stake? Is the eternal well-being of billions of people actually hanging in the balance? Is God being mocked? Are we that far from what our Founding Fathers intended?*

Without a doubt.

But there is good news. A generation of passionate patriots are arising who, like David of old, believe enough in the cause of Christ to risk everything to see it restored.

Consider a more complete version of Patrick Henry's previously mentioned speech and allow its passion to saturate your soul:

If we mean not basely to abandon the noble struggle in which we have been so long engaged, and which we have pledged ourselves never to abandon until the glorious object of our contest shall be obtained, we must fight! I repeat it, sir, we must fight! An appeal to arms and to the God of hosts is all that is left us! They tell us, sir, that we are weak; unable to cope with so formidable an adversary. But when shall we be stronger? Will it be the next week, or the next year?... Shall we gather strength by lying on our backs, and hugging the delusive phantom of hope, until our enemies shall have bound us hand and foot? **Sir, we are not weak if we make a proper use of those means which the God of nature hath placed in our power... There is a just God who presides over the destinies of nations... The battle, sir, is not to the strong alone; it is to the vigilant, the active, the brave...**The war is inevitable—and let it come! I repeat, sir, let it come.

It is in vain, sir, to extenuate the matter. Gentlemen may cry, peace, peace but there is no peace. The war is actually begun!... Our brethren are already in the field! Why stand we here idle? What is it that gentlemen

wish? What would they have? Is life so dear, or peace
so sweet, as to be purchased at the price of chains and
slavery? Forbid it, Almighty God! I know not what
course others may take; but as for me, give me liberty
or give me death (emphasis mine).[5]

That, my friend, is a man with a cause. Henry loved freedom
and believed in God's destiny for America! We must be like-
minded; just as he and his patriot counterparts stated, we must
fight! Though our weapons and enemies are spiritual, the war is
equally as real and the stakes just as great. The soul of a nation
and the cause of Christ on earth are on the line.

Greatness is found when American character and American
courage overcome American challenges. When Lewis Morris of
New York was about to sign the Declaration of Independence,
his brother advised against it, warning he would lose all his
property. Morris, a plain-spoken founding father, responded
"…Damn the consequences, give me the pen." That is the
eloquence of American action.[6]

Morris displayed the heart of a cause-minded David staring
down the mocking "Goliath" of his day. We must do the same.
Our giants are humanism, liberalism, abortion, immorality, drugs,
breakdown of the family, materialism, love of pleasure, human
trafficking, fatherlessness—make your own list. But without
question, this generation is awaiting today's Patrick Henry's and
Lewis Morris's. We need warriors who will stand up, accept the
challenge, grab their pens, and write history.

I pray that America finds heroes such as these once again…
and I pray we resurrect our song.

PART II

THE WEAPONS

CHAPTER 5

THE GLOVES

I was in route to Beersheba, Israel, waiting to change planes in the huge international wing of the Istanbul Ataturk Airport. A little groggy from a 14 hour, overnight flight, I sat down to take a break. Then the unexpected show began. A young man stripped to only his underwear and began parading past me and others who sat nearby. I was astonished. *Am I hallucinating?* was my first thought. A quick shake-of-my-head later, I realized I was very lucid and watching a live, R-rated version of "Strutting Your Stuff in the Istanbul Airport."

And strutting he was. Definitely not drunk, this demonized man was parading like a runway model. I tried not to stare—we all did—as he made two passes in front of me before security personnel arrived and led him away.

I live an interesting life.

I will never fully understand demons—I suppose in one sense, that's good—but this manifestation I did understand. It was an in-your-face act of spiritual warfare, related to the purpose of my journey. The kingdom of darkness was putting me on notice that they knew my plans and were going to resist me as much as possible.

Regarding my adventurous trip to Beersheba, here is some background information. My pilgrimage was related to an important dream a friend of mine had in 2007 about taking out giants, which, as I mentioned in the Introduction, I wrote about in my book, *An Appeal to Heaven*.

In the dream, I was a boxer and fought five giants in five rounds, knocking out each of them—one per round. I floored each giant with one punch; and with each opponent, I alternated fists.

After I knocked out the fifth giant, I walked out of the ring and addressed the young man having the dream. Holding up my gloved fists, I declared, "If you're going to take out the giants in this season, you're going to have to wear these two gloves." One of the gloves had the word "Everlast" on it; the other read "Evergreen."

Interesting.

I would find the meaning of this dream in the life of Abraham and an encounter he had with Jehovah at a place called Beersheba. I extensively studied this event in Abraham's life and as God began prompting me early in 2017 that the time of fulfillment was at hand, Holy Spirit led me back to this event in Abraham's life. As I studied it once again, I desperately wanted to possess the fullness of revelation represented by the two gloves, Everlast and Evergreen. I then heard Holy Spirit say something completely unexpected, "I not only want you to visit Beersheba in the scriptures, I want you to visit it literally. Go to Beersheba and get the gloves."

Some revelation is costly.

So I made my plans, hopped on an airplane and off to Beersheba I went.

The Weapon of Everlast

Everlast is one of the most common names in boxing equipment. The word "Everlast" meant more to me than just boxing equipment, however. I knew there was a scriptural connection, and I knew what it was. True to form, the Lord had been paving the way for me so I would recognize it at the right time. Back in 2007 when the dream occurred, I had been studying the life of Abraham and his journey with God. In Genesis 21:33, scripture tells us that at Beersheba, Abraham called on "the Everlasting God." The Hebrew name is *Olam El*, and it's the first time in scripture anyone used *Olam El* as one of God's names.

The meaning of the word *olam* is not our typical concept of eternity, which is basically "an endless future." The concept of *olam*, however, is eternity extending *both* directions in time. One lexicon described it as the most distant times in both directions—past and future. Even such an amazing description as that falls short, however, because the word "times" in the definition violates the very concept of *olam*, which is timeless. *Olam* cannot be confined to a timeline. This is why the word was applied to God. *Olam El*, Everlasting God, created time and exists outside of its boundaries and limitations.[1]

Mind boggling, I know.

For our finite, human minds—and in order for us to understand why Abraham chose this phrase to glorify God—suffice it to say that *Olam El* is the strong and mighty God, who is Lord over the past, present, and future. He can completely forgive and heal the past, and can predict the future with 1,000 percent accuracy.

For example, God doesn't see a born-again, former prostitute as "a former prostitute;" He doesn't see the redeemed murderer as "a former murderer." When He forgives, He eradicates past sins and separates them from us "as far as the east is from the west" (Psalm 103:12). He cleanses us and remembers our sins no more (Hebrews 8:12, 10:17). *Olam*, through the cross, eradicates all record of our former sins.

Abraham's Failures

Consider Abraham's situation when he calls on the Lord as *Olam El*, Everlasting God. He has been on a twenty-five year journey of attempting to follow God, and as he looks back over his life, Abraham remembers occasions where he failed miserably. There were blotches, torn places, and embarrassing failures on his timeline.

Most believers think of Abraham as "the father of faith," a description of him taken from Romans 4:16. Likewise, Hebrews 11 refers to him as a great man of faith. We forget, however, Abraham wasn't a man of great faith in portions of his life. There were significant deviations from that path which could have disqualified him.

Actually, Abraham and Sarah both wavered at times in their attempt to believe God would give them a son. The Lord had promised them children, but when no child came, their lack of faith in God's promise caused them to introduce Hagar into the family, resulting in the birth of Ishmael, another sin that could have disqualified them. Later, they actually laughed a cynical laugh at God's final re-stating of the promise. And why not? Abraham was 99 years old and Sarah was 90 (Genesis 17:1,17).

This wasn't Abraham's only failure of faith, however. On two different occasions when Abraham and Sarah were younger, he was afraid that foreign kings might kill him in order to marry her. His solution for these predicaments included the despicable acts of pretending Sarah was his sister rather than his wife. In essence, he threw Sarah to the wolves in order to save his own life. She was, indeed, taken into the harem of both kings, two more incidents that could have stolen their destinies! God, however, supernaturally intervened before physical unions occurred. These deceptions and fabrications were horrible breaches of

the marriage covenant and bold-faced lies—ones I'm sure neces-
sitated awkward conversations with the kings when Abraham
had to set the record straight. He and Sarah probably had a few
things to work out, as well.

Olam Overcomes Our Unrighteous Past

Having committed such despicable acts, why does the Bible call
Abraham a father of faith and a friend of God? Because even
though he may not have fulfilled these descriptive phrases at every
phase of his journey, they are accurate descriptions of how he
finished. Abraham "*grew* strong in faith" (Romans 4:20, italics
added), and in his walk with God. And having been cleansed
by *Olam* of his sinful past, Abraham isn't remembered as "the
covenant breaker," "the liar," or "the double-minded man." He
is known as God's friend and our faith example!

Abraham was grateful his past actions were not allowed to
define his present situation. *Olam El* had navigated him through
every season—even the embarrassing and wicked ones—and
preserved his destiny. And as He does for all of us, He reached
back in time and cleansed Abraham's wrongs, once and for all.

With that in mind, one can almost see Abraham as he
searches for the right name to use in thanking and glorifying
God. Elohim? Adonai? Yahweh? None described the God who
controls time—past, present, and future. Finally, exhausting all
known possibilities, he had to coin a new name. In Abraham's
mind, the process may have been something similar to this:

> *You are more than* Yahweh, Adonai *and* Elohim. *You
> are the infinite and powerful God of the Ages—Olam
> El. You are outside of time and Lord over time! As
> Ruler over the past, present and future, you forgave and
> eradicated my sins and kept my destiny intact. When I
> was unfaithful, You were faithful; when I doubted, You
> overcame my unbelief; when I lied, You were able—not*

only to forgive me—but to cleanse me and keep my marriage intact. And even when our bodies were too old to conceive and reproduce—99 and 90 years of age—You placed some of Your timeless nature in Sarah and me, and we drank from the fountain of youth. Truly, You are the creator of and ruler over time—Olam El, Everlasting God!

With that declaration, Abraham entered a new phase in his walk with God. He recognized that the Sovereign who was *bigger than his past*, could be *fully trusted with his future*. Abraham placed his faith in Olam El, the God who could bring his fractured past into alignment and chart the right course for his destined future.

Wearing the Glove for America

When I pray for revival in America, I boldly and confidently wear the Everlast glove. I know the breaches in America's history well—the injustices, the evil acts, and our many sins. Like Abraham, we have failed, sometimes egregiously. But I also know *Olam El* and what He can do through the blood of the cross. No giant is too big for Him, including those empowered by our sin.

Yes, our nation has a flawed past and perhaps an even more flawed present. But I'm not asking for a merit-based revival where God gives us tokens of His goodness in response to our excellent behavior. Obviously, the Lord isn't going to award America with a revival simply because He's impressed with our actions. But isn't that the point of revival? If we were "good enough," we wouldn't need one!

I'm asking for awakening because covenant-keeping *Olam El* lives up to His name. I have faith for revival because I know the timeless God can reach back and heal our breaches. I declare that Everlasting God can cancel the bad fruit, repairing the wrongs we're responsible for and also the ones we've inherited. Forgiveness and cleansing—redemption—are His specialties. When we wear this glove and place our faith fully in God's grace and the blood of Jesus alone, blessings can and will flow through America's timeline once again.

The Weapon of Evergreen

In Genesis 21:33, the same verse in which Abraham called on *Olam El*, he also planted an *evergreen* tree. Obviously, I had read this verse often enough to remember that Abraham planted a tree before calling on *Everlasting God*. I just didn't know a tamarisk tree was an evergreen! He planted an *evergreen tree* and called on the *Everlasting God*. Abraham wore both gloves of my dream.

Why did Abraham plant that type tree? Memorials or monuments were extremely important in his day, as they were used to remind people and nations of significant events. Evergreen trees symbolized covenant. When Abraham planted the evergreen tree, he was establishing a witness or memorial to his covenant relationship with Everlasting God. The message through the planting of this tree was: "*Olam* has proven Himself faithful to His covenant with me time and time again. I now declare my covenantal faithfulness to Him. I will forever honor my allegiance to Everlasting God."

When Holy Spirit mentioned "Evergreen" in the boxing dream, He was pointing America back to covenant with Him. If we would once again honor our promises to *Olam*, returning to the God of our fathers; if we would return to God's original purpose and plan for America, partnering with Him in His cause of redemption throughout the world, then the faithfulness of Everlasting God would be demonstrated, delivering us from the giants ravaging our land.

When people live in covenantal faithfulness to God, not only are they blessed but their children and grandchildren are, as well.

This has certainly been the case with America. We have been extremely blessed by the covenant keeping of the generations before us. Each succeeding generation, however, must wear its own covenantal glove.

America will win the battle with today's giants if we, like Abraham and our forefathers, wear these two gloves. If we return to a faith that God's redeeming power is bigger than our weaknesses and failures, we will defeat the over-fed giants of our day. If we can believe that through the blood of Jesus, God's covenantal mercy triumphs over judgment (James 2:13), and He who began a good work in us can finish it (Philippians 1:6), then we'll prevail.

CHAPTER 6

USING HISTORY AS OUR WEAPON

I hated history class in school. I must have had boring teachers—it couldn't have been my shallow thinking. I'm not sure when this changed for me but it most certainly did. And if you suffer from the same issue I was plagued with back in my high school days, well, I'm about to help you!

In previous chapters we have studied the question David asked before he faced Goliath: "Is there not a cause?" We've also discovered that the Hebrew word translated "cause," also means "history." Therefore, David was very possibly asking his brother and fellow Israelites, "Is there not a history to write?" But David may also have been referring to past history. "Don't we have enough history with God to give us confidence in His faithfulness? And are there not promises from Him in our history that we can stand on?" Roots are essential; foundations are critical.

Can we win today's battle with our yesterday? We can. Actually, we *must* use history to fight our battles and take out today's Goliaths. As we will see in the next chapter, David's most powerful weapon when facing Goliath was, in fact, his history. I can almost hear the shock in some of your cynical, history-adverse minds. Nonetheless, it is true. Before exploring this, however, let's find out what makes history so powerful. This will make David's story much more meaningful.

In my book *An Appeal to Heaven* I mention an important phrase spoken to me several years ago by Holy Spirit: "the synergy of the ages." This phrase was shared with me during a season when Holy Spirit was emphasizing the importance of connecting with past generations. In short, the synergy of the ages is *multiplied power through generational agreement and honor*.

Scriptures clearly teach that the generations are connected, with both blessings and curses flowing from one generation to the next (see Deuteronomy 5:9, 7:9). Like it or not, Adam's sin—and resulting sin nature—was, in fact, passed on to you. God sees the generational connection so literally that He routinely makes a promise to one generation, knowing it won't be fulfilled until a future generation (see Hebrews 11:39-40). Bloodlines are so connected spiritually that the tithe Abraham paid to Melchizedek was credited to his great grandson, Levi: "…through Abraham even Levi…paid tithes," (Hebrews 7:9). What my ancestors have done—my family history—affects me, and what I do impacts those who come after me. That is staggering in its ramifications!

Put Yourself In The Storyline

The power and importance of understanding this connection to history can be seen through a stirring dream given to Julie Meyer, an internationally known worship leader and seasoned intercessor. As the dream began, Julie saw 7 ambulances lined up, each with lights flashing. Growing very concerned, she walked to the back of one of the ambulances to see what was happening. When she looked in, Julie saw a non-responsive person laying on a gurney. Next to the patient was an attendant working feverishly to revive him.

Julie immediately knew the attendant was an angel. He looked at her and said, "I can't find a heartbeat." She went from one ambulance to the next, finding the same scenario—patients on gurneys with angels attending them, trying to restart their hearts. Suddenly, one of the angels looked directly at Julie and confided, "It's the intercessors."

The despondent condition of the intercessors made sense to me. For a number of years, I have watched as the strength of the prayer movement has waned, many becoming weary, disillusioned, with little motivation. Many intercessors have prayed years for revival, but revival hasn't materialized, and some of them have experienced what Proverbs 13:12 refers to as "hope deferred." And as this passage teaches, hope deferred has made their hearts sick. Traveling across America, I can attest to the truthfulness of the dream. It's challenging to find a heartbeat in many weary and hopeless intercessors.

As Julie's dream continued, suddenly one of the angels shouted, "I found a heartbeat, but it's very faint!"

The other angels grew excited and inquired, "What did you do?" They, of course, wanted to use the same procedure in order to generate a heartbeat in their lifeless intercessors.

The first angel's response was surprising. "Tell the old stories. When I started telling her stories of what God did in the past, her heart began to beat."

With that, these heavenly attendants began speaking to the intercessors about the First Great Awakening, the Second Great Awakening, and other Holy Spirit outpourings—right up through the healing revivals and tent meetings of the 1940's, 50's, and 60's. As they did so, the hearts of all the intercessors started to beat again. At this point in the dream, an angel looked at Julie and insisted, "Tell the old stories of what God has done in the past."

When I first heard the entire dream, it impacted me. However, this angelic messenger then added instructions that stirred my heart even more: "Tell the intercessors to put themselves in the storyline, because the old stories are also their stories." What a profound and intriguing thought.

Who among us really thinks this way? But we should. God has one overarching plan for humankind; we're all part of the same unfolding drama. Our generation's role in history is simply another act of yesterday's play; our battles are conflicts in one ongoing war. Every revival in history is but a sequel in Holy Spirit's ongoing series of outpourings, and every soul saved enters the same spiritual family. *Our stories, though many, are one.*

Put yourself in the storyline, because the old stories are actually *your* stories!

Synergy, Not Segmentation

For too long, we Christians—even those who are students of church history—have viewed accounts of past moves of God as something to be taken out of a box once in a while and dusted off for observation and sentimentality. We love those old stories, but we certainly don't think of them as something we can agree in prayer with, connect to, or draw strength from. And we've certainly never thought of them as *our* stories. They are past tense, a dead history. I had never thought of Wesley and his Methodists as my movement. Finney's awakening certainly hadn't been my awakening, and William Seymour's Azusa Street outpouring wasn't claimed as mine. Most of us simply don't think that way.

Our shortsighted reasoning has stolen from us the synergy of the ages. We've not put ourselves in the storyline. Since we don't typically align with past movements or agree with past prayers, this has all too often led to the *segmentation* of the ages, forcing each generation's intercession and effort to stand on its own. Actually, the results are more devastating than that: God says that when the generations disconnect, it creates a curse (Malachi 4:6).

However, putting ourselves into the storyline God is writing allows us to tap into the strength and life of what He did years ago. We begin to understand the *eternal* purposes of God, not just the purposes we feel are for our present time. When we do this, He then can continue through our generation what He began with previous generations. And again, according to Hebrews 11:40, those who came before us can finally see their promises fulfilled, while watching from the balcony of Heaven.

Reinforced by Julie's dream, this revelation opened my heart to a myriad of storylines we, as a generation, needed to identify with. History came alive. I knew we could insert ourselves into the storyline of Charles Finney, believing that city-changing revivals would be rekindled in our day. We could agree with the powerful prayers of Rees Howells for revivals that would shake nations. We could join the efforts of Martin Luther King, Jr., and see his dream of racial healing in America reach its intended goal. The great cloud of witnesses had finally become more than mere spectators and cheerleaders to me; they were an earlier leg of a relay race, waiting for someone to grasp their baton.

This truth pierced my conscience. God began the process of connecting my heart and actions with those who had lived before me. My life began expanding, being defined not just by an eighty or ninety-year destiny, but also by an inter-generational purpose. I realized I was part of a historical chain, planned by God and built with human lives. "Back to the future" took on new meaning: Like Elijah's servant, Elisha, I would need to connect with the past in order to find my future. The power Elisha needed today was hidden in his yesterday (2 Kings 2:14-15). Reaching back would not only bring added significance to my life, but also to the lives of those who had lived before me (Hebrews 11:39-40). And God's love of relational connection would find fulfillment, causing Him to release an entirely new level of spiritual power—the synergy of the ages.

Incredible.

Putting Myself Into America's Storyline

I immediately began processing this revelation in the context of my calling to America. It was obviously relevant to praying for nations. I now could connect with America's story more personally, joining my heart to the prayers and dreams of pilgrims, colonists, pioneers, and every other generation our story is made from.

Whatever the cost, I determined to do my part in keeping the dream alive.

When David said, "Is there not a history?" he was doing more than remembering; he was referring to more than the preserving of historical roots. *David was reaching back, putting himself in the storyline.* He was declaring that promises made by God hundreds of years earlier were his guarantee of victory today. David was staking his faith on the synergy of the ages… and he knew the stone would find its mark.

Keep reading and I'll prove it.

CHAPTER 7

DAVID'S HISTORY

The first thing God tells us in the story of David and Goliath is the location of the battle.

> "Now the Philistines gathered their armies for battle; and they were gathered at Socoh which belongs to Judah, and they camped between Socoh and Azekah, in Ephes-dammim. Saul and the men of Israel were gathered and camped in the valley of Elah, and drew up in battle array to encounter the Philistines" (1 Samuel 17:1-2).

I realize that doesn't interest you. You're like me: *Come on, Holy Spirit, get to the good stuff: Goliath's description; the drama of his taunts; the fear of the Israelites; David, the young sheepherder; the battle; off with the giant's head.* I skipped those two boring verses for the first 60 years of my life.

And missed a nugget.

This location was in the territory of Judah, which was the tribe David belonged to. Holy Spirit was informing us, right from the start, that *this land belonged to David and his tribe.* It had been given to them by God generations ago. David had more than *squatter's* rights to the property the giant was trying to claim; he had *divine* rights. The first two verses of the story assure him of victory—period. The God who created and owns the earth (see Psalm 24:1) had the right to give it to whomever He pleased. And in history, He had given it to the tribe David belonged to.

Battle over.

Don't think so? I'll give you another reference that reinforces this truth. When Nehemiah was allowed by the Persian King Artaxerxes to return to Jerusalem in order to rebuild its walls, he faced great opposition. The locals, led by Sanballat, Tobiah, and Geshem, despised the Jews and were determined to stop them from building. When Nehemiah faced their threats and opposition, he stated his case for success in one verse, "I answered by saying, 'The God of heaven will give us success. We his servants will start rebuilding, but as for you, you have no share in Jerusalem or any claim or *historic right to it*'" (Nehemiah 2:20, NIV, italics mine).

"I have a historical, God-given right to this city," Nehemiah declared. "You don't. Therefore, I win, you lose." Case closed.

It is beyond doubt that God raised up America for His purposes. I will say more in the next chapter regarding our God-given history. For now, however, suffice it to say that He owns America, just as He does the entire earth; and in that right of ownership He delegated stewardship of this nation to followers of Christ, believers who would partner with Him in His great cause of redeeming the world.

If the body of Christ in America is ever able to fully grasp this revelation, the giants attempting to steal our nation have no chance.

Uncircumcised Philistine

David's next "history weapon" can be seen in the fact that not once did he call Goliath by name. He referred to him only as the "uncircumcised Philistine." What is *that* all about? Try as I may, I can't imagine two guys about to fight and the taunt of one to the other is, "You're uncircumcised."

As strange as this seems, there was actually a good reason. In David's day, circumcision was one of the primary signs that a man was in covenant with God. Since the days of Abraham this had been the case. It was a requirement mandated by God, obviously for health purposes. Circumcision served the added purpose, however, of being a picture of New Testament believers who would have the "flesh" of our hearts circumcised (see Romans 2:28-29).

For our purposes in this discussion, however, what we must understand is that David was stating to the giant, "My acceptance of and obedience to the precepts of the Abrahamic covenant means I'm in covenant with God; you're not. Since those in covenant with one another share enemies, you'll be fighting God, not just me. This battle won't be decided by your size, experience, weaponry, or strength. It was decided a long time ago, and I'm going to defeat you with my covenantal history. I win; you lose."

No wonder secularists want to steal America's God-given history. We shouldn't be surprised that former President Obama once said we were not a Christian nation, contending that we were also a Muslim nation, a Hindu nation, an atheist nation, and so on.[1] Karl Marx once said, "The first battlefield is to rewrite history."[2] The demons in Marx knew the power of history. And demons today inspire anti-Christ forces in America to try and rewrite our history, as well. As believers, what we must do is stake our claim to the fact that God birthed America and we are in covenant with Him. If we war using this truth, He will fight for us and we will defeat the giants.

Personal History with God

David wasn't finished brandishing his history, however. Not by a long shot. After asking, "Is there not a history?" he began recounting his *personal* history with God. David spoke of God's supernatural ability imparted to him when facing a lion (1 Samuel 17:34-36). "I seized him by his beard, attacked him, and rescued the lamb," he said. As if that wasn't amazing enough, David also killed a bear! "The LORD who delivered me from the paw of the lion and from the paw of the bear, He will deliver me from the hand of this Philistine," David decreed (verse 37). This small, physically insignificant young man, had faith that was anchored—not to his own abilities—but to a history of God's faithfulness.

It's important to know that David stated that history. He said it. After teaching on the power of history recently, I was asked by a Messianic Jewish rabbi if I knew the meaning of the Hebrew word for "testimony." I did not.

"The word doesn't mean simply to convey something from the past," he informed me. "Its true meaning is 'to repeat an action or do it again.' We Hebrews believe," he continued, "that when we share about what God did in the *past*, it releases the same power into the *present*…in other words, power is released to 'do it again.'"

Whoa!

My head was spinning.

He continued, "That's one of the reasons we share with our children the stories of what God did in our Hebraic history. It's not only so they'll know their cultural history; it is so the power in that history can be released to them today. For example, when we tell them about Passover and the Exodus, we believe God's delivering and saving power that was demonstrated back then, will be released to save and deliver our children from bondages they may have today."

Whoa times two!

The rabbi went on to tell me he and his congregation had been experiencing healings from simply sending other believers to sick individuals and having them recount healings they had received in the past. When they testified of their healings, power was released to "do it again."

This drove me to my lexicons. While studying the word "testimony," which meant exactly what the rabbi had said, one dictionary sent me to the Hebrew word for "remember." Similarly, it doesn't mean simply to think about something from the past; it means to *do* what is being thought about.[3] This is why God tells us in Isaiah 43:26, "Put Me in remembrance..." He doesn't require this because He, like us humans, sometimes needs a reminder. Rather, He is instructing us to ask Him, based on something said or done in the past, to take action today.

God "remembered" Hannah, who had been barren, and she conceived (1 Samuel 1:11). He "remembered" His covenant with Abraham, Isaac, and Jacob, and commissioned Moses to deliver the Israelites from Egyptian slavery (Exodus 2:24). For God, *remembering* moves Him to action.

This was life-changing revelation for me. I finally understood why God said we overcame satan by "the word of [our] testimony" (Revelation 12:11). And I knew why David *stated* his testimony of the lion and the bear!

After doing so, David then did something extremely interesting. He grabbed his staff, five stones and his sling, and approached the giant (see 1 Samuel 17:40). Why would David want to be encumbered with his staff when fighting Goliath? In those days, men carved symbols depicting their history on their staffs; it was their journal, of sorts. David's staff no doubt depicted pictures of a dead lion and dead bear—his testimony, his history.

Who knows what other victories it pictured? Perhaps it had the phrase "God is my father" inscribed. Many scholars believe David was conceived "illegitimately," that his father

Jesse had an affair with a maid and David was the result. They believe this is why Jesse didn't invite him to the line-up of his sons, from which Samuel planned to choose Israel's next King. When asked if there were any other sons, most translations say Jesse referred to David as the "youngest" (1 Samuel 16:11). The word is actually *qatar*, however, and means "of no account; not worthy."[4] David was an outcast. He stated in Psalms 27:10, "My father and my mother have forsaken me, but the LORD will take me up."

David refused to allow the rejection by his parents and half-brothers to define him. He also refused to allow Goliath to define him. "I choose, rather, to honor my history with God, who has become my Father, and from Whom I receive my identity," David implied in the Psalms. And when facing Goliath, he declared his testimony, grabbed his history (staff), and headed toward the battle. This is so incredibly profound.

The Power of Testimony

David made one stop on the way to the battle, visiting a nearby brook to gather stones as ammo for his sling. Even this seemingly insignificant act was connected to history. In this passage, the Hebrew word used for "brook" means "inheritance."[5] That may seem strange, but Hebrew is a pictorial language, and this word pictures *receiving something, then possessing the authority to control where it goes;* thus, an "inheritance," or a "streambed." Actually, it is perfectly logical for Holy Spirit to use this symbolic picture of an "inheritance." After all, it WAS David's land, his inheritance. David took his "history" in one hand, reached into his "inheritance" with the other, then ran to face the giant.

WOW!

And yet, there is still one more connection to his history David used in this battle with the giant: his Judah nature. Most Christians believe Judah means "praise." That, however, is a derived meaning. In this pictorial language, the Hebrew word pictures the extending of the hand. It is, therefore, the word for "praise," since raising the hands is a form of praise.

Because Judah means to extend the hand, however, it also means "one who throws a stone."[6] In his history, David was from "the tribe that throws stones!" He probably thought, *I don't need a sword or spear. I'm from the tribe that throws stones. All I need to do is reach deep into my DNA, my history, and be who God made me to be—a stone thrower. If I do, I'll defeat the giant.*

We believers in America are going to defeat the giants ruling our nation, and we will do so using the same weapon David used: *our history*. The God who formed and preserved America in her past will fight for her today. As you pray for our nation, boldly declare His past faithfulness, believing in the power of testimony.

To help fill your arsenal, let's take a look at some of America's auspicious God-given history.

CHAPTER 8

AMERICA'S HISTORY

God raised up America for the same general purpose He had in mind when He birthed Israel: redeeming the world from Adam's fall. Though our specific role is clearly different from theirs—Israel was destined to be the people through whom Messiah would come to earth—the end game was the same. Both nations were called and destined by God to help Him save the world from sin and reunite His earthly family to Himself.

In order to facilitate this holy calling, God was directly involved in the birthing, molding, and shaping of the USA. This doesn't mean He approved of all of our actions throughout history, such as broken covenants or treaties with the Native tribes, slavery, abortion, and other grievous sins. Yet, in spite of these evils, America, like Israel, exists for His holy purposes and Jehovah has been involved with us throughout our history.

Though America grants freedom of religion and beliefs to all, this must never alter our identity and does not change our calling. We must never lose sight of our purpose and destiny, nor should we ever apologize for it. America doesn't exist to further Islam, Hinduism, Buddhism, or any of the other religions of the world. Their followers are welcome here, but these religions are not our identity. We are called by Jehovah God, the God of the Bible, to partner with Him and His Son, Jesus Christ, whom the Bible teaches is the only way to God (John 14:6; Acts 4:12).

This certainly doesn't mean we should be arrogant or intolerant. Likewise, we should never try to force our beliefs on others. To the contrary, Christ—through love and the inherent power of the gospel—desires to *win* people to Himself; and He intends for us, His church, to be His instrument in doing so. Nevertheless, though we are inclusive, tolerant and welcoming of all, we must never abandon our calling nor forget our rich Christian heritage.

A City On A Hill

From the days of the pilgrims, godly men and women have believed the Almighty was involved in the birth of our nation. They also felt if a nation chose to partner with and honor God, that nation would experience His favor and blessing in extraordinary ways. Washington and the colonial dreamers agreed, believing the Sovereign was, indeed, birthing "a city [nation] set on a hill that can't be hidden…a light to the world" (Matthew 5:14). They no doubt knew of John Winthrop, a leader of the puritan's Massachusetts Bay Colony, using this verse in his 1630 speech on board the Arbella to describe what he believed God wanted to build in America.[1]

The Founders knew about the planting of the cross at Cape Henry in 1607, and the ensuing prayer meeting dedicating the land to God's glory. They had read the Mayflower Compact of 1620, stating the voyage was made "for the glory of God, and advancement of the Christian faith…"[2] Would God honor these events and prayers? Even more importantly, was He inspiring these actions? Was America truly God's dream, not just theirs? They believed it was.

The pilgrims and our Founding Fathers absolutely believed America had a God-given destiny. Throughout our history, America's presidents and leaders have reiterated this belief. John F. Kennedy referenced Matthew 5:14 and Winthrop's famous speech, as did Ronald Reagan and numerous other U.S. Presidents.[3] Though modern day revisionists try to rewrite and remove our history, the truth will always trump their lies.

The Declaration of Independence

As our Founders declared their independence from England, they also acknowledged their dependence upon God. Fully aware that He was the Author of their national existence, they relied on Him to also provide the necessary wisdom to create and maintain this new nation. The Declaration of Independence, our original founding document, has 4 clear references to God: it speaks of Him as our Lawmaker, Creator, Judge and Protector. The Declaration concludes with these words:

> For the support of this Declaration, with a firm reliance on the protection of Divine Providence, we mutually pledge to each other our Lives, our Fortunes, and our sacred Honor.[4]

After signing the Declaration, some wept. Others, like Witherspoon, bowed their heads in prayer.[5] Samuel Adams rose and stated, "We have this day restored the Sovereign, to Whom alone men ought to be obedient. He reigns in heaven and…from the rising to the setting sun, may His Kingdom come."[6]

What an encouraging and amazing history to connect with and build on!

Washington's Heart After God

These men weren't confused about whether or not they wanted God—the Judeo-Christian God of scripture—to be involved in this nation. Nor was George Washington. Note his God-honoring statement at his inauguration as the first president of the United States on April 30, 1789:

> ...It would be peculiarly improper to omit in this first official Act, my fervent supplications to that Almighty Being who rules over the Universe, who presides in the Councils of nations, and whose providential aids can supply every human defect, that his benediction may consecrate to liberties and happiness of the People of the United States... No People can be bound to acknowledge and adore the invisible hand, which conducts the Affairs of men more than the People of the United States. Every step, by which they have advanced to the character of an independent nation, seems to have been distinguished by some token of providential agency... We ought to be no less persuaded that the propitious smiles of Heaven, can never be expected on a nation that disregards the eternal rules of order and right, which heaven itself has ordained.[7]

I love the fact that Washington spoke not only of *acknowledging* God's hand in our nation but of *adoring* Him. Indeed, there is a history of dependence on God and of His faithfulness toward this nation. Hundreds of examples could be cited. Apart from Jehovah's sovereign help, England would have crushed these floundering revolutionaries. Our forefathers were not perfect, but they were God-honoring, and His overruling role in their lives cannot be denied.

John Adams

Bringing the Sovereign into our founding, John Adams said that the day on which the Declaration of Independence was signed:

> Will be the most memorable…in the history of America. I am apt to believe that it will be celebrated by succeeding generations, as the great anniversary festival. It ought to be commemorated, as the Day of Deliverance, by solemn acts of devotion to God Almighty. It ought to be solemnized with pomp and parade, with shows, games, sports, guns, bells, bonfires and illuminations, from one end of this continent to the other, from this time forward forevermore.
>
> You will think me transported with enthusiasm, but I am not, I am well aware of the toil and blood and treasure that it will cost to maintain the Declaration, and support and defend these States. Yet through all the gloom I can see the rays of ravishing light and glory. I can see that the end is worth more than all the means.[8]

The Liberty Bell

The Liberty Bell, which rang on the day of America's birth, got its name from the Bible verse inscribed on it (yes, the Liberty Bell contains a verse of scripture): "Proclaim liberty throughout the land to all the inhabitants thereof" (Leviticus 25:10). This verse is taken from the description of the year of Jubilee, which was a prophetic picture of Christ, our Jubilee, who forgave our debts and freed us from spiritual slavery. Just to make sure you get the connection—our nation's birth was announced under the biblical decree that "Christ is our Liberator and Savior!"

Humanists, atheists, and liberals may not like facts such as these, but as John Adams once said, "Facts are stubborn things…"[9]

Our nation's form of government was actually taken from scripture. "The Lord is our Judge [Judicial Branch]...Lawgiver [Legislative Branch]...and King [Executive Branch]" (Isaiah 33:22). Now, there is a weapon to use when you pray for our government! Decree that God will once again be honored as Judge, Lawgiver, and King.

America's Colleges

One hundred and six of the first 108 colleges in America were founded on our Christian faith.[10] Students at Harvard were required to read the scriptures twice daily.[11] Harvard's founders stated, "All knowledge without Christ is vain;" its motto was, "For Christ and the church."[12]

The rules and precepts of Harvard stated that, "Every student shall consider the main end of his study is to know God in Jesus Christ..."[13] Princeton's motto was, "Under the protection of God she flourishes."[14] Jonathan Dickenson, the first president of Princeton stated, "Cursed be all learning that is contrary to the cross of Christ."[15]

Countless other examples could be given. "Under God" is more than a religious quote stuck in the Pledge of Allegiance to satisfy America's Christian zealots. It is fact...it is our history. We can lay claim to it and, like David, *we can war with it*.

As you pray for America, declare and decree that we are a Christian nation. State your faith in the God who keeps covenant and shows mercy. Ask Him to restore our true purpose and calling. Decree that as our Lawgiver, Judge, and King, He will rule our nation. Worship Him as our Founder and Savior.

Refuse to allow lying historians, secularists, and polytheists to steal America's history and purpose!

through laws, decrees, and righteous judgments, kings presented heaven's rule *to earth.* Melchizedek was uniquely both.

Christ, The Fulfillment

As such, this king and priest was a type of Christ, THE King-Priest. Jesus is King over all the earth, as well as the High Priest of all believers. Consistent with the functions of these two roles, as King He represents the rule and authority of God to earth, and as our High Priest, Christ represents our needs Godward. He is, indeed, both the Lion and the Lamb.

The scriptures teach, however, that Christ would not fulfill these functions single-handedly. In both the Psalms (110:4) and the book of Hebrews (5:6 and 7:17), Jesus is spoken of as leading an "order" of priests. Yet 1 Peter 2:9 also calls them a "royal priesthood." As members of Christ's body and extensions of Him, the Head, we are partakers of His King-Priest ministry (see Hebrews 3:14; 2 Peter 1:4; John 14:12). All that He is, He is through us.

As Christ's priestly intercessors, we represent the needs of people to God. In His name, we petition heaven on behalf of them, asking for God's mercy, forgiveness and provision. In my book *Intercessory Prayer*, I share the story of a young girl who was in a coma with irreversible brain damage. She had been in this condition for 1½ years when Holy Spirit sent me to pray for her. For over a year I visited her weekly, and interceded for her. I wept, petitioned the Father for a miracle, worshipped over her, and prayed for her in my prayer language. This was all priestly intercession.

After just over a year, the Lord visited this young girl in the hospital room and gave her a new brain. What an amazing miracle it was! And what an honor to be used in this way by the great High Priest, Jesus.[1]

There have been other times in my representation of Christ that I've functioned in the Kingly, ambassadorial role. In those cases, I didn't *petition* heaven, I *commanded*—for that is what the Greek text communicates in the Lord's Prayer—Christ's Kingdom to come and His will to be done (see Matthew 6:10).

In 1980, I was asked to pray for a newborn baby with a fractured skull. During a difficult birth, the doctor had used forceps to deliver the baby, and in the process had inadvertently fractured his skull. As I began to pray, Holy Spirit led me to command healing into this infant's skull. I decreed that in the powerful name of Jesus, the baby's skull was being healed.

It happened instantly! Through this miracle the mother was born-again and at church the following Sunday I had the privilege of dedicating this baby to Jesus.

That is kingly intercession.

Priests request; kings command and decree. Priests pray; kings rule. Priests operate in humility, kings in boldness. We must function in both aspects of these callings, just as Christ does. David, though a great worshipper and intercessor, wasn't modeling priestly activity when he faced Goliath; he was demonstrating kingly authority.

The Family and The Ekklesia

Both of these aspects can be seen in Christ's great declaration of Matthew 16: "I also say to you that you are Peter, and upon this rock I will build My church; and the gates of Hades will not overpower it. I will give you the keys of the kingdom of heaven; and whatever you bind on earth shall have been bound in heaven, and whatever you loose on earth shall have been loosed in heaven" (Matthew 16:18-19).

When Jesus said he would "build" His church, the word is *oikodomeo*. The basic concept of the word is building a family, not a building. It implies the creating of a lineage, the establishing of a family or building of a household.[2] In this one word, Jesus was declaring that He had come to reclaim God's family.

As believers and part of this family, we relate to God as Father. We honor Him as such, love and serve Him, and trust our heavenly Father to meet our needs. We "offer up" (see 1 Peter 2:5) worship, love, and requests just as any child would to his or her parents. We also offer up petitions on behalf of others. This is priestly activity.

The next word Jesus used, however, carries in it the kingly concept: "I will build My *church*." The Greek word is *ekklesia*. Contrary to what most believe, the Church isn't a building, an organization, a congregation, or a worship service. In Christ's day, to both Greeks and Romans, an *ekklesia* was a governmental assembly. It was a ruling body, a legislature.[3]

The Romans actually included the concept of discipling in *ekklesia*—shaping the thinking of nations. The governmental teams Rome sent to conquered regions in order to rule them, (*ekklesias*) were also charged with the responsibility of changing the culture of those regions. Romans knew that through this, they could keep conquered nations from rebelling and attempting to re-establish their former identities. Their goal was to make them think like Romans in all facets of life!

The concept of an *ekklesia* being a government body is why Jesus, when stating that He would build His *ekklesia*, went on to say they would be given the keys (authority) of His kingdom government. He also stated that they would bind (*deo*) and loose (*luo*). These are legal terms, meaning "to forbid" and "allow," "to legally restrain," and "legally liberate."[4] This is also why Jesus said the "gates of hell," a phrase meaning "the government of hell," would not stop His *ekklesia*—His Kingdom government—on earth.

Let The Church Be The Church

The kingly aspect of the body of Christ is simply the Church functioning as the Lord intended—as His *ekklesia*. Many in the body of Christ have made progress in functioning as priests,

75

though perhaps not always at the level we should. We have NOT, however, learned to function well as His royal ambassadors.

This is about to change. The church is moving into a new era—the fresh age of the Melchizedek order. Just as Christ modeled, we will function as priests, representing the needs of people heavenward; but we will also move in His authority, commanding heaven's will earthward. We will cast out demons, speak life to dead and diseased bodies, and even, at times, control the forces of nature.

And, like David, we will take out the giants.

There is a new breed of warrior arising in the earth. Worshipping warriors. Priestly warriors, but warriors, nonetheless. They will know their authority as emissaries of the King, and as representatives of heaven's kingdom on earth. These ambassadors will issue heaven's commands over nations, people groups, and individuals. They'll be Christ's *ekklesia—liberators,* deliverers, and enforcers.

Like David, these bold believers will fear no evil. Like Caleb, they'll *request* giant infested regions as their assignment. Like Jesus, they will walk in such dominion that principalities will tremble when they enter a region.

Consider the following report shared by George Otis, Jr., in his book *Informed Intercession*:

In the 1970's Almolonga, Guatemala was idolatrous and economically depressed. Alcoholism was rampant; poverty and violence the norm. Families suffered terribly due to the depravity that ruled. The gospel did not prosper; persecution of Christian leaders was common.

In 1974, a series of five-hour prayer vigils began, and shortly thereafter God began to move. Deliverance and healings began to break forth, even resurrections from the dead. Conversions began to take place at such a rate that 90 percent of the 19,000 people in the Almolonga are now evangelical Christians.

The revival has impacted every area of life: families, businesses, even the produce of the land. Now nick-named "Guatemala's Vegetable Garden," the fields produce three harvests per hear, with five-pound beets, carrots bigger than a man's arm and cabbages the size of basketballs.

Crime disappeared so much that, in 1994, the last of the four jails closed.[5]

Testimonies such as this will become common in the fresh age of the Melchizedek order. The Church, Christ's *ekklesia,* is moving into her finest hour.

Step up, royal priest. Get your gloves on, grab your inher-itance and your history, and slay your giant.

ENDNOTES

Chapter 2

1. CBSNews. "Best Songs of the Century?." CBSNews.
   com, March 8, 2001. www.cbsnews.com/news/
   best-songs-of-the-century/
2. McClean, Don. "American Pie." Universal Publishing
   Group, 1971.
3. National Right to Life. "Abortion Statistics, United States
   Data and Trends." NRLC, 2018. www.nrlc.org/uploads/
   factsheets/FS01AbortionsintheUS.pdf
4. Center for Medical Progress. "Investigative Footage."
   CMP, 2015-2018. www.centerformedicalprogress.org/
   cmp/investigative-footage/
5. Ibid.
6. National Institute of Mental Health. "Suicide." NIH,
   2015. www.nimh.nih.gov/health/statistics/suicide/index.
   shtml
7. RAINN. "Children and Teens: Statistics." RAINN, 2018.
   www.rainn.org/statistics/children-and-teens
   RAINN. "The Criminal Justice System: Statistics."
   RAINN, 2018.
   www.rainn.org/statistics/criminal-justice-system

8. Dudley, Susan. "Teenage Women, Abortion, and the Law." Prochoice, September 2015. Prochoice.org/wp-content/uploads/teenage_women.pdf

9. Centers for Disease Control and Prevention. "Reported STDs in the United States." CDC, November 2015. www.cdc.gov/std/stats14/std-trends-508.pdf

10. U.S. Department of Justice. "Special Report." U.S. Dept. of Justice, September 1988. www.fathermag.com/news/1780_stats.shtm/

11. Warner, Jennifer. "US Leads the World in Illegal Drug Use." CBSNews, July 2008. Cbsnews.com/news/us-leads-the-world-in-illegal-drug-use/ Family Safe Media. "Pornography Statistics." TopTenREVIEWS, Inc., 2007. www.familysafe.com/pornography-statistics/

12. Pew Research Center. "Religious Landscape Study." Pew Research Center, 2018. www.pewforum.org/religious-landscape-study/

13. Barna. "The State of the Church 2016." Barna, September 2016. www.barna.com/research/state-church-2016

14. Barna. "Most American Christians Do Not Believe that Satan or the Holy Spirit Exist." Barna, April 2009. www.barna.com/research/most-american-christians-do-not-believe-that-satan-or-the-holy-spirit-exist

15. Ibid.

16. Barna, George. *Boiling Point.* (Ventura, CA: Regal Books, 2001). p.80.

17. Twain, Mark. *Mark Twain on Common Sense: Timeless Advice and Words of Wisdom from America's Most-Revered Humorist.* (New York, NY, Skyhorse Publishing, Inc., 2014).

18. Larson, Craig Brian. *Illustrations for Preaching and Teaching.* (Grand Rapids, MI: Baker Books, 1993). p.123.

Chapter 3

1. Larson, Craig Brian. *Illustrations for Preaching and Teaching.* (Grand Rapids, MI: Baker Books, 1993). p.222.

2. Strong, James. *The New Strong's Expanded Exhaustive Concordance of the Bible, Red-Letter Edition.* (Nashville, TN: Thomas Nelson Publishers, 2001). Reference no. 1697. Zodhiates, Spiros. The Complete Word Study Dictionary. (Iowa Falls: IA: Word Bible Publishers, 1992). p.1838.

3. Strong. Reference no. 1555 and 1540.

4. Larson, Craig Brian. *Illustrations for Preaching and Teaching.* (Grand Rapids, MI: Baker Books, 1993). p.21.

5. Kann L., McManus T., Harris, W.A., et. al. "Youth Risk Behavior Surveillance, United States, 2015. MMWR Surveillance Summaries, 65 (6), 2015. p.26. www.cdc.gov/healthyyouth/data/yrbs/pdf/2015/SS6506_updated.pdf
Minnesota Department of Health. "About STD Awareness Month: April is National STD Awareness Month in Minnesota." MN Dept of Health, 2017. www.health.state.mn.us/div/idepc/dtopics/stds/stdmonth/stdmonthfacts/html

6. Center for Medical Progress. "Investigative Footage." CMP, 2015-2018. www.centerformedicalprogress.org/cmp/investigative-footage/

7. Larson, Craig Brian. *Illustrations for Preaching and Teaching.* (Grand Rapids, MI: Baker Books, 1998). p.235.

Chapter 4

1. Metzger, Bruce M. *The Bible in Translation: Ancient and English Versions.* (Grand Rapids, MI: Baker Academic, 2001). p.124.

2. Marshall, Peter and Manuel, David. *The Light and the Glory*. (Grand Rapids, MI: Fleming H. Revell, 1977). p.271.

3. Copeland L., Lawrence, L.W., McKenna S.J. *The World's Greatest Speeches*. 4th ed. (United States: Dover Publications, Inc., 1999). p.232-233.

4. Brokaw, Tom. *The Greatest Generation*. (New York, NY: Random House, 1998). p.18.

5. Copeland et. al. p.232-233.

6. Bush, George W. *Celebration America's Spirit Together: The 54th Presidential Inauguration*. Iain Lemos edition. (Epicenter Communications, Inc., 2001). p.4.

Chapter 5

1. Strong, James. *The New Strong's Expanded Exhaustive Concordance of the Bible, Red-Letter Edition*. (Nashville, TN: Thomas Nelson Publishers, 2001), Reference no. 5769.

Chapter 7

1. Obama, Barack. "'Call to Renewal' Keynote Address." Washington, D.C., June 2006. www.obama.senate.gov

2. Washington, Ellis. *The Progressive Revolution: History of Liberal Fascism Through the Ages, Volume V, 2014-15 Writings*. (Lanham, MD: Hamilton Books, 2017). p.219.

3. Strong, James. *The New Strong's Expanded Exhaustive Concordance of the Bible, Red-Letter Edition*. (Nashville, TN: Thomas Nelson Publishers, 2001). Reference no. 2142.

4. Zodhiates, Spiros. *The Complete Word Study Dictionary*. (Iowa Falls: IA: Word Bible Publishers, 1992). p.2012.

5. Strong. Reference no. 5157 and 5158.

6. Ibid., Reference no. 3034.

Chapter 8

1. Winthrop, John. "A Model of Christian Charity." 1630.
2. Mayflower Compact. 1620.
3. Kennedy, John F. "The City Upon a Hill." Speech Given at Massachusetts General Court. January 9, 1961
   Reagan, Ronald. "We will be a City Upon a Hill." Speech Given at the First Conservative Political Action Conference. January 25, 1974.
   Also quoted by Presidents John Adams, Alexander Hamilton, George Washington, James Madison, Abraham Lincoln, Ulysses S Grant, Woodrow Wilson, Calvin Coolidge, Franklin D Roosevelt, and Bill Clinton.
4. The Declaration of Independence. July 4, 1776.
5. Marshall, Peter and Manuel, David. *The Light and the Glory.* (Grand Rapids, MI: Fleming H. Revell, 1977). p.307.
6. Ibid., p.309.
7. Washington, George. "Washington's Inaugural Address of 1789, a Transcription." National Archives and Records Administration. www.archives.gov/exhibits/american_originals/inaugtxt.html
8. Marshal and Manuel. p.310-311.
9. Adams, John. "Argument in Defense of the British Soldiers in the Boston Massacre Trials." December 4, 1770.
10. McCalman, Allison. "The History of Christian Education in America." Classroom, 2018. https://classroom.synonym.com/the-history-of-christian-education-in-america-12080826.html
11. Richard, Carl J. *The Founders and the Bible.* (Lanham, MD: Rowman and Littlefield, 2016). p.16.

12. Ahrens, Darrell J. *Divine Love/Divine Intolerance.* (Oakland, OR: Elderberry Press, Inc., 2009). p.283.
13. Ibid.
14. Princeton University. "University Flag, Shield, and Motto." Princeton University, 2017. www.princeton. edu/~oktour/virtualtour/korean/Info09-Flag.htm
15. Thwing, Charles Franklin. *American Colleges, Their Students and Work. 2nd ed.* (New York, NY: G.P. Putnam's and Sons, 1883). p.56.

Chapter 9

1. Sheets, Dutch. *Intercessory Prayer.* (Bloomington, MI: Bethany House Publishers, 1996). p.19-22.
2. Strong, James. *The New Strong's Expanded Exhaustive Concordance of the Bible, Red-Letter Edition.* (Nashville, TN: Thomas Nelson Publishers, 2001). Reference no. 3618.
3. Ibid. Reference no. 1577.
4. Ibid. Reference no. 1210 and 3089.
5. Otis Jr., George K. *Informed Intercession.* (Ventura, CA: Regal Books, 1999.)

ABOUT THE AUTHOR

Dutch Sheets is an internationally recognized teacher, conference speaker, and best-selling author. He has written over twenty books, many of which have been translated into more than thirty languages. His international bestseller, Intercessory Prayer, has sold over a million copies worldwide and is being used to empower believers for passionate prayer and societal transformation.

Seeing America experience a sweeping revival and return to its Godly heritage is Dutch's greatest passion. He is a messenger of hope for America, encouraging believers to contend for awakening in our day and reformation in our lifetime.

Dutch and Ceci, his wife of over 40 years, live at the base of the Rocky Mountains. They enjoy reading a good book, long walks in the woods, and spending time with their grandchildren.

To learn more, visit www.dutchsheets.org.

OTHER BOOKS WRITTEN BY DUTCH SHEETS

An Appeal to Heaven

Authority in Prayer

Becoming Who You Are

Dream

El Poder de la Esperanza

The Essential Guide to Prayer

God's Timing for Your Life

History Makers

How to Pray for Lost Loved Ones

Intercessory Prayer

Intercessory Prayer Study Guide

Intercessory Prayer, Youth Edition

La Oracion Intercesora

The Pleasure of His Company

The Power of Hope

Releasing the Prophetic Destiny of a Nation

The River of God

Watchman Prayer

The Way Back

MONTHLY PARTNERSHIP

Dutch Sheets Ministries
Monthly Partnership Program

We invite you to join us in carrying God's
message across this great nation.

With each monthly donation of $50 or more
you will receive:

- **Dutch Sheets' latest teaching**
- **A monthly letter from Dutch Sheets Ministries**
- **Valuable gifts and resources**
- **Special discounts to our online store**

Partner with us to bring awakening and revival
to America. Together, we can do it again!

To learn more about our
Ministry Partnership Program, visit
www.dutchsheets.org.